TERRIBLE TWINS

igloo

Have you ever seen two such loveable twins? They're very hard to tell apart.

This is Tara and that is Tamara. Er, no . . . that's Tara and this is Tamara.

Hold on; that's Tony and this is Tiny. Oh, I don't know, it's so confusing. That's why their mum calls them her Terrible Twins.

As they grew up, they were always being mistaken for each other.

But there was one big difference between them. . .

Tamara was good and Tara was very naughty.

If Tamara tidied up their bedroom, then Tara would go straight in and trash it.

Then Tara would pretend to be Tamara, so that their mum didn't know which one to be angry with.

By the time they went to school, there was only one thing they didn't argue about. They both hated their nickname.

"Don't call me Terrible," moaned Tamara. "I'm not like her."

"Yeah," agreed Tara, sticking out her tongue. "She's nothing like me. She's a goody-two-shoes."

The next minute they would be scrapping on the living room floor.

One day their mum asked them to cycle down to the Post Office to buy some stamps.

Tara jumped on Tamara's bike and shot off. "Hey!" shouted Tamara giving chase. "Give me back my bike, you thief!"

As Tara raced ahead she saw Fussy Florence carefully washing her dad's car. Tara rode straight through a puddle, splashing thick muddy water on both Fussy Florence and the car.

"Oh, no!" she screamed. "Look what you've done. I'm going to tell your mum."

Tamara stopped to help but Fussy Florence was too angry. "Just go away, you Terrible Twins."

The girls carried on and cycled into the park. Tara spotted old Mrs Bulgebottom with her dog, Fang.

Tara sneaked up behind them and untied the dog's lead. Fang barked twice and ran through the flowerbeds as he chased after a squirrel.

Tara rode away laughing across the grass with the Park Keeper chasing after her. "Can't you read the signs?" he shouted, waving his fists in the air.

Tamara finally caught Fang and returned him to his angry owner.

Tamara found Tara at the fruit market. She was cycling in and out of the stalls. "Be careful," Tamara called out after her. "You'll have an accident."

But Tara was going too fast. She bumped into a man who was just putting the last apple on the top of his display. He toppled over, knocking his stall onto the floor.

People began tripping and sliding on the fruit. Soon, everyone, including the Twins, was on the floor.

Tara was first up. She snatched her bike that was on top of the pile and rode off.

Tamara stayed behind to help tidy up the mess. Then she got on her bike and rode home, too.

Later that day, Florence, Mrs Bulgebottom, the Park Keeper and the lady from the Post Office were standing in front of the Twins complaining to their mum.

They were all talking at once. "There she is, she's the one that did it."

"No, not her. It was the other one."

No one could make up their minds. It looked as if Tara was going to get away with it.

There was just no way to tell which Twin had caused all the trouble.

Suddenly the Park Keeper raised his hand. "I remember now," he smiled. "It was the girl on the blue bike."

Everyone agreed; the girl on the blue bike was the culprit.

Mum was amazed as she turned to look at Tamara. "That's your bike, isn't it?"

"Well, it is," mumbled Tamara. "But Tara was riding it."

"What a Terrible thing to say," everyone exclaimed. "You shouldn't blame your sister," and Tamara was sent up to her room for the rest of the day.

"But . . . but, that's not fair," Tamara stammered.
"No arguing," scolded her mum, pointing her finger upstairs.

As Tamara trudged out of the room everyone thanked Tara for being so helpful.

Tara's mum gave her a big kiss, but as she hugged her, she noticed something odd.

"Why is your dress so wet and muddy?" she asked.

"Well," stammered Tara, "It's like this...

also available...

Rude Roger   Dirty Dermot   Pickin' Peter   Space Alien Spike   Silly Sydney   Nude Nigel

Shy Sophie   Cute Candy   Royal Rebecca   Grown-up Gabby   Terrible Twins   Show-off Sharon